The Fourth Chester Book of Motets
Revised Edition

The German School
for 4 voices

Edited by Anthony G. Petti

LIST OF MOTETS

CHESTER MUSIC
part of WiseMusicGroup

EXCLUSIVELY DISTRIBUTED BY

FACTUS EST REPENTE

Suddenly there was a sound from heaven like a rushing mighty wind. (*Acts. II, 2.*)
Strengthen, O God, what you have made in us, from your holy Temple in
Jerusalem. (*Ps. 67, xxix-xxx.*)

Gregor Aichinger (1564 – 1628)

5

REGINA CAELI

Queen of heaven, be joyful, alleluia, for he whom you were worthy
to bear has risen as he promised: pray for us to God, alleluia.

Gregor Aichinger (1564 – 1628)

8

REGINA CAELI repete ut supra

REGINA CAELI repete ut supra

ECCE CONCIPIES

Behold, you shall conceive and bear a son, and you shall name him Jesus.
He shall be great and called the Son of the Most High. He shall govern
the throne of David and his kingdom, and rule in the house of Jacob for
ever; and his kingdom will have no end. (*Luke,* I, 31-3.)

Jacob Handl (1550 – 1591)

10

ECCE QUOMODO

See how the just man dies, and no one feels for him in his heart. The just are taken away and no one cares. The just man is borne from the presence of evil, and his memory shall be held in peace. His dwelling place is in peace, and his abode is in Sion.

Jacob Handl (1550 – 1591)

RESONET IN LAUDIBUS

Let Sion resound with the joyful acclaim of the faithful: he whom Mary bore has appeared. The prophesies of Gabriel have been fulfilled. The Virgin has given birth to God as divine mercy willed. Today a king has appeared in Israel, born of the Virgin Mary.

Jacob Handl (1550 – 1591)

CANTATE DOMINO

Let all the earth sing God a new song. Sing to the Lord and bless his name:
proclaim his salvation from day to day. Declare his glory among the nations,
his wonders among all peoples. (*Ps. 95, i – iii*)

Hans Leo Hassler (1564 – 1612)

20

LAETENTUR CAELI

Let the heavens rejoice and earth be glad, the sea in her fulness respond:
the fields and all that is in them will be happy. Then all the trees of the
woods shall rejoice before the face of the Lord, because he comes: for
he shall come to judge the world with justice and the people with his
truth.   (*Ps. 95, xi – xiii.*)

Hans Leo Hassler (1564 – 1612)

TU ES PETRUS

You are Peter, and upon this rock I will build my church, and the
gates of hell shall not prevail against it. (*Matthew.* XVI, 18.)

Hans Leo Hassler (1564 – 1612)

25

26

PUER NATUS

A boy is born in Bethlehem, therefore rejoice Jerusalem.
He lies within a manger, who lives for ever.
Kings from Saba came offering gold frankincense and myrrh.
There is joy on this birthday, let us bless the Lord.
May the Holy Trinity be praised, let us give thanks to God.

Michael Praetorius (1571 – 1621)

SALVE REX NOSTER
(Salve Regina)

Hail to our King, father of mercy, our life, sweetness and hope.
To you we cry as exiles, children of Eve; to you we offer our
sighs, lamentations and weeping in this valley of tears. Turn then,
as our advocate, your eyes of mercy towards us, and after this exile
show us Jesus, your only-begotten son. O clement, loving and sweet
King, Jesus, hail.

Salve Regina, attrib. Adhemar de Monteil, Lutheran adaptation.

Michael Praetorius (1571–1621)

DEUS IN ADJUTORIUM

O God, come to my aid, Lord, hasten to help me. Let them be ashamed and
confounded that seek to possess my soul. Let them be put to flight and thrown
in confusion who wish me harm. Let them be turned back in their shame who
scornfully laugh at me.   (*Ps. 69. i-iii.*)

Ludwig Senfl (c. 1499 – c. 1555)

VERBUM CARO

The Word was made flesh and dwelt amongst us, whose glory we
have seen as being the only - begotten of the Father. (*John, I, 14.*)

Johann Walter (1496 – 1570)

EDITOR'S NOTES

While the madrigal is now coming into its own in terms of individual editions and collections, the motet is still somewhat neglected, and has even suffered a setback, because the disappearance of Latin from the Roman Catholic liturgy has caused many works to go out of print. Musicologists continue to introduce new editions, but their main emphasis is on the provision of larger scale works for the concert hall or of scholarly editions which are often beyond the scope of the average choir to decipher and transpose, let alone sing.

The aim of the present series is to make more readily available a comprehensive body of Latin motets from the Renaissance period, combining old favourites with lesser known or hitherto unpublished works. The first five volumes are arranged nationally, covering Italy, England, Spain, Germany and Slavic areas, and the Low Countries, each containing, on average, twelve motets drawn from not less than six composers. They are for four mixed voices, and should all be within the scope of the reasonably able choir. They also provide a fair selection from the liturgical year, as a guide for the church choir and for performing choirs who like to present their music according to theme or season.

The editor has endeavoured to preserve a balance between a critical and a performing edition. The motets are transposed into the most practical performing keys, are barred, fully underlayed, provided with breathing marks, and have a reduction as a rehearsal aid. Editorial tempi and dynamics are also supplied, but only in the reduction, leaving choirmasters free to select their own in the light of their interpretation of a given piece, vocal resources and the acoustics. The vocal range for all parts is given at the beginning of each motet.

As an aid to musicologists, the motets, wherever possible, are transcribed from the most authoritative source, and the original clefs, signatures and note values are given at the beginning and when they change during the course of a piece. Ligatures are indicated by slurs, editorial accidentals are placed above the stave. The underlay is shown in italics when it expands a ditto sign, or in square brackets if entirely editorial.

Each volume includes a brief introduction concerning the scope of the edition, with notes on the composers, the motets, the sources, editorial emendations and alterations, if any, and a table of use according to the Tridentine Rite.

Both the quality and quantity of Latin church music in Germany were somewhat impaired by the Reformation, though publication of Latin works was not so severely curtailed as in England. Many of the German States remained Catholic, while a number of Lutheran composers, for instance, Walter, Hassler and Praetorius, used Latin texts as well as the vernacular. No Catholic German composers of the period have the stature of a Palestrina or a Lassus, but the best of them are extremely able, and deserve a higher reputation than they have today. There are also many distinguished composers who come within the ambit of the Holy Roman Empire, though they are really Austrian, Swiss, Bohemian or, like Handl, Slovene. Thus, all in all, there is still an impressive corpus of Latin church music from Germanic sources, and certainly a considerable amount set for four mixed voices in a comfortable range.

The first composer represented here, Gregor Aichinger (1564-1628), was a Catholic priest and organist to the highly influential merchant-banker family of the Fuggers in Augsberg. He published several volumes of sacred music, which are typified by liveliness, imagination, clarity of outline and brightness of tonal colour. He was also one of the first German composers to use a *basso continuo*.

Until the language of the liturgy changed to the vernacular, his double motet, *Factus Est Repente* and *Confirma Hoc* was understandably one of the most popular settings of the text, being a favourite piece for the feast of Pentecost and confirmations. It was published in *Fasciculus Sacrarum Harmoniarum Quatuor Vocum*, 1606. The traditional elements of plainsong and the fugue constitute an important part of the framework of the motet, but are made to be fully expressive of the spirit and meaning of the text. The opening (which resembles that of Aichinger's six-part *Intonuit de Caelo*) uses the plainsong motif in fugal style, but the treatment is *stretto*, animated and percussive, giving the impression of the suddenness and force of the wind from heaven. The descent from heaven is indicated by the first note of "caelo" being the highest in the phrase, followed by a drop of at least a third and a long undulating but falling melisma. The fugue is repeated and swiftly concludes in an emphatic and almost homophonic passage. The second section, "tamquam advenientis", symmetrically balances the first, and begins in much the same way, though from the lower parts upwards. It also uses the same short, repeated, notes in a style reminiscent of the Venetian. The fugue follows a very climactic sequential patter, with the cantus firmly leading the other parts into the cadence for "vehementis", much as the tenor did for the final "de caelo". For the invocation which begins Part Two, Aichinger uses a double canon, one (between the cantus and tenor) being a psalm tone in augmentation, the other performing an arabesque but serene descant. Then comes an exciting combination of two themes: "a templo sancto tuo", chiselling in music the solid blocks of temple stone, while "quod est in Jerusalem" seems to sound out a joyful carillon.

The *Regina Caeli* is one of many motets which Aichinger wrote in honour of the Blessed Virgin. He provided at least two for each of the four seasonal Marian anthems, including two settings of the *Regina Caeli*. The one given here is the simpler and shorter. It is compact and unaffected, though affording scope in echo effects and dynamic range, if so desired by the performers. The motet conveys a loose paraphrase of the plainsong version, as do most settings of the anthems. It is mainly homophonic and monosyllabic, with melismas reserved for key words (e.g., "laetare" and "portare"), and what fugal passages there are, are very brief, the most extensive use being saved for "ora pro nobis" in the final section, as might be expected. Aichinger keeps the texture suitably light, the bass occuring only sparingly in the verse, though all four voices are employed continuously in the refrain to provide a rich, full harmony. The use of a refrain after each verse is unusual in the anthems, and is certainly unliturgical, but is nevertheless artistically satisfying. Both *Factus Est Repente* and *Regina Caeli* are in the Ionian mode, a popular one with Aichinger, and apparently suited to his musical temperament.

Jacob Handl (1550-1591), sometimes known by the Latin form of his name, Jacobus Gallus, was born at Reifnitz, Carniola, but spent most of his life in Bohemia. He was a member of the Vienna Court Chapel for a time, then chapel master to the Bishop of Olomouc, and from about 1568 spent the rest of his life in Prague. Handl's style varies considerably. He wrote large-scale works using double choirs in the Venetian manner, and intricate, harmonically sophisticated motets with abundant chromaticism; but he could also write entirely chordally, in a simple and highly economical vein. The three motets published here are in this last category. Two of them are completely homophonic, and the third, *Ecce concipies*, almost entirely so. They make their impact mainly by sonority, suddenly modulated chords for important verbal phrases and syllables, and by a wonderful sense of speech rhythms and verbal accentuation.

All three works were originally published in *Opus Musicum*, a four-volume collection of motets for the liturgical year, the first and third being contained in *Tomus Primus* (1586) and the second, *Ecce Quomodo*, in *Tomus Secundus* (1586). *Ecce concipies*, though a short motet, is in two parts, the second beginning with "Super solium", where the liturgical text naturally divides for the versicle. It is mainly in the transposed Ionian mode, though it really has a feeling for keys, and resembles F major (here transposed to E♭ major) with frequent tonal modulation. The opening has a gentle but brief double canon, the alto and bass paired in unadorned progressions, and the cantus and tenor in more elaborate style, with a pleasing melisma for the most important syllable of "concipies". The next section, "et paries", contains the last of the fugal writing, and terminates with melismas similar to those of "concipies", again for the most important syllable. Thereafter, the treatment is homophonic, but with considerable variety of rhythm and pace, and sudden modulation to produce some striking chords, the flattened D and raised A and E being most common (originally all a tone higher). At one stage ("Hic erit"), Handl uses only the three upper voices in a highly emotive pattern of rising and falling six-three chords, the risk of cloying being dispelled by the final syncopation of the tenor. Text repetition is common to give a sense of climax reinforced in the second repeat of "Filius Altissimi" by the high tessitura. The final "non erit finis" makes its point by a fourfold repetition, together with the staccato emphasis conveyed by the short note values. Amongst the rhythmical variants is the quick triple section for "Super solium", a technique common in the period, but fitting naturally the contours of the text.

The Tenebrae responsory *Ecce Quomodo* is a masterpiece of simplicity, and an eloquent refutation of the frequently voiced opinion that Renaissance motets never had strong emotional content (another splendid example being Jaquet of Mantua's *O Jesu Christe*). It is set in aBcB form and, like *Ecce Concipies*, is formally divided into two, "In pace" being liturgically the verse, after which the "et erit in pace" of the responsory is repeated — the pattern for all the Tenebrae responsories. The main feeling of the motet is that of a touching but well controlled threnody. Lugubriousness is avoided by keeping a fairly strong sense of the major and by maintaining the pace throughout, though with eloquent silences between phrases, and a fermata before the second section. The force of lamentation is conveyed by highlighting the most telling emotive words and phrases: for example, "moritur", "percipit corde", "tolluntur", "iniquitatis", "sublatus est justus" (the most striking in the whole motet), "pace" and "memoria". The emphasis on these words is achieved in a variety of ways. First, the most important syllables are double the length of the normal note unit, or at least dotted ("memoria"). Next, the stressed syllable is usually at the highest point of the phrase in all or most of the parts (e.g., "moritur"). Sometimes, the emphasis is achieved by syncopation, especially by accenting the weak part of the beat ("percipit", bars 7 and 10). Text repetition also reinforces the emotional effect, as in "percipit corde", "et in Sion" and "et erit in pace". Most effective of all are the sudden modulations, the chief example being in three of the chords for "sublatus est justus", and the Db major chord for the stressed syllable of "memoria". The mood of the whole piece is subtly varied, from the grief of the first section, through the quiet resignation of "et erit in pace", to the almost triumphant affirmation of "et in Sion". It is probable that Handl intended antiphonal effects in the repeated phrases, and these are suggested editorially in the reduction.

Resonet in Laudibus was one of the most popular Renaissance Christmas carols, with many variants for both the words and the tune. A number of German and Flemish composers provided settings, and Handl composed at least three: a six-part, a five-part, and the four-part included here (all published in the first volume of *Opus Musicum*). The text for all three settings is the same until the last line, which in the six-part is "per Mariam virginem est natus Rex", and in the five-part, "quod annunciatum est per Gabriel". The Handl settings have the identical antiphonal division into *tutti* and *alternatim* (*alternatim* being replaced in this edition by "Choir 1" and "Choir 2"). The melodic line carried in the cantus, is also basically the same in all three, though is least ornamented in the four-part version. The work has a vibrant triple rhythm (here translated into 6/4 time) which is both majestic and sprightly, maintaining its impetus to the end. The three lower voices act mainly as an accompaniment, but have interesting, imaginative and agile contours, especially in such passages as "Eia, eia", where each has an independent rhythm. As ever with Handl, the harmony, more in the key of F major than in the transposed Ionian mode, modulates boldly and effectively, with a subtle alternation of F♯ with F♮ natural and B♭ with B♮. The motet can be interpreted in a variety of ways, and considerable experimentation with echo effects is possible. Although the present edition follows the composer's apparent instructions for the disposition of the different choirs, the following alterations to his scheme are suggested as being particularly effective: bar 14, Choir 2 or Quartet; bars 20-22, Choir 1; bars 23-6, *Tutti*; bars 27-9, Choir 1; bars 30-2, *Tutti*. One of the major differences in this rearrangement is the use of full choir for "Hodie apparuit", which is surely the climax to this superb piece.

Hans Leo Hassler (1564-1612) was born in Nuremberg of a very talented musical family. Early in life he went to study under Andrea Gabrieli in Venice and became a colleague of Giovanni Gabrieli. Returning to Germany, he obtained the post of organist to the Fuggers, and in 1602 was appointed Chief *Kapellmeister* in Nuremberg. He wrote a large number of sacred and secular works and organ compositions. Like Handl, whom he resembles stylistically in many ways, Hassler uses a variety of techniques in his sacred compositions, some of them clearly derived from Giovanni Gabrieli, being especially evident in his polychoral compositions, and a few others taken from the Flemish composers. Though Hassler and Handl are similar, Hassler seems to be a much more extrovert and forthright composer, with a strong feeling for well-sustained and pleasing melodies, while Handl is rather more subtle and less flamboyant. The three pieces transcribed here (all published in *Sacri Concentus*, 1601 and 1612) are in contrasting styles. The first, *Cantate Domino*, one of three settings by Hassler, is a lively, mainly homophonic motet with considerable momentum and skilfully varied rhythms. It moves from duple to triple time and back to duple, and contains a moderate amount of syncopation to maintain the interest and give a sense of springy accentuation. It also modulates quite frequently from C major (originally F major) to the related keys of G and F. Although the words are treated mainly monosyllabically, there are some nicely flowing melismas, "Cantate" being particularly suitable for such treatment. The original clefs suggest that the piece was intended for four lower voices, but it works very well when raised a fifth to accommodate SATB treatment.

Laetentur Caeli is in an early Baroque style, with a predominance of short notes used mono-syllabically, (including the demisemiquaver when the original notation is halved) quick turns, and rapid syncopation, which features are especially prominent in Giovanni Gabrieli. An antiphonal effect is provided by the uses of duets and trios, giving the impression of much larger vocal resources. A change to and from triple time takes place much as in *Cantate Domino*, but the duple time is so varied that the regular *tactus* evident in the preceding motet seems subservient to the general continuity of movement in which the quavers busily convey the sudden springing into life of all nature to greet the Messiah.

The third Hassler motet, *Tu es Petrus*, returns to an earlier Italian style typical of Palestrina, and indeed, the opening fugal phrase is reminiscent of ones used in a number of Palestrina's motets. The fugue is very skilfully handled and sustained, and all the new subjects are clearly articulated. As in the Palestrina style, there are many textual repetitions, expressed in sequential patterns which follow the acceptable polyphonic melody curve, even if they are occasionally a little more balletic than the strictly traditional style would permit. From "et porta inferi", Hassler introduces pairs and trios, but reverts to a more fugal style for "adversus eam". In the last half of the motet echoes of Palestrina's six-part setting occur quite strongly, though Hassler's motet still preserves its individuality.

Michael Praetorius (1571-1621), the greatest of the Lutheran composers, held several important Kapellmeister positions, including ones at Lüneberg and the court of the Duke of Brunswick. His publications of choral music in Latin and German are voluminous, quite apart from his instrumental music and his most famous work, *Syntagma Musicum*. For all his prolificness, it has not been possible to provide a fair sampling of his works in this collection, for few of his works are set as four-part Latin motets. However, the first work, *Puer Natus* (from *Musae Sioniae*, 1607) is a typical example of Praetorius's art in arranging Christmas Carols. This highly symmetrical and rhythmical carol (known in German as *Ein Kind Geborn*) was extremely popular, and Praetorius set it in many different ways, using both the German and Latin texts. This is his most compact setting, but is nevertheless provided with inventive and swift accompaniment, requiring an especially alert bass line.

The second Praetorius piece, *Salve Rex Noster* (from *Eulogodiae Sioniae*, 1611) is an interesting example of a Lutheran modification of a Latin liturgical text to remove the Marian content and replace it by references to the Deity exclusively. Since Praetorius follows the plainsong of the solemn *Salve Regina*, it is possible to reconstruct what the underlay of the original text would have been, and this has been supplied editorially for those who wish to perform the work as a Marian anthem. Praetorius has not only closely observed the original plainsong, carried by the cantus in augmentation, but has also retained the same musical divisions by use of fermata, rest or double bar. Understandably, the setting is homophonic throughout, for the text is especially long. However, to counteract the somewhat marching movement of the cantus, Praetorius has ensured that the parts do not progress uniformly to the same syllables. The rhythms of the individual lines vary, and frequently contain some swift Early Baroque figures. All the lower parts, in particular the bass, are also given a great deal of movement. The work is somewhat opaque and could become turgid in a poor performance, but it has a great sense of majesty, and the harmonies are very rich and sonorous.

Although he is usually claimed as a German composer, Ludwig Senfl (c.1499-c.1555) is now known to be Swiss, having been born in Basle. His dates have caused almost as much dispute as his nationality, and a common present-day alternative is c.1486-1542 or 3. Usually hailed as the greatest German Catholic composer of the early 16th century, Senfl studied under Isaac, and succeeded him as master of the imperial chapel in Vienna. He later became court conductor at Munich, where he died. Senfl's works are copious, even by Renaissance standards, and include masses, motets, music for the liturgical offices, and secular songs. He was Luther's favourite composer, and the two corresponded, but there is no evidence that Senfl composed sacred works expressly for him. Although his sacred music was very popular, it sometimes strikes modern ears as austere and overly controlled. These features are apparent to some degree in his *Deus in Adjutorium*, which is Part I of a double motet (Munich, Bayerische Staatsbibliothek, Mus. MSS. 10, ff,101-9; *Liber Selectarum Cantionum*, 1520, no. 6). The opening fugue, based on the plainsong intonation, builds up very slowly, and for much of the time there are bare octaves and fifths. Senfl is also sparing in the use of all four parts, much as Josquin des Près is. But he then moves to a fine sense of climax for "Euge, euge" which is the high point in the motet, where the inner parts lead the others in the cry of scorn, each line descending a third, in a style of writing which Lassus was to exploit with magnificent economy in such works as *Justorum Animae* (cf. "sunt in pace").

The last composer in this collection is Luther's close friend, Johann Walter or Walther (1496-1570). In his early years he sang in the court choir of Frederick of Saxony, and then became bass cantor in the Torgau choir. Among his later musical posts was that of Kapellmeister to the Elector of Saxony (1548-54). One of Walter's main achievements was assisting Luther in establishing the German mass, and the bulk of his compositions are in the vernacular. Nonetheless, he wrote a number of Latin works, including *Verbum Caro Factum Est*, published in the 1551 edition of *Geystliche gesank Buchleyn*. As is common with many of Walter's motets, the tenor maintains the plainsong *cantus firmus* throughout in augmentation. The other parts have brief points of imitation, but otherwise weave their independent way in a very smooth pattern of melodious melismas.

Table of use according to the Tridentine Rite

Motet	liturgical source	seasonal or festal use
Factus Est Repente	1st & 2nd ant. Matins; Commun. & Offert., Pentecost	Pentecost; Votive Mass Holy Spirit Confirmation
Regina Caeli	Easter anthem of Blessed Virgin	Easter; Bl. Virgin
Ecce Concipies	1st respon., 1st Saturday of Advent (Prague (Breviary)	Advent
Ecce Quomodo	6th respon. Matins, Holy Saturday	Passiontide, Lent
Resonet in Laudibus	(Christmas carol)	Christmas
Cantate Domino	Ps. Matins, Christmas Day	Christmas; General
Laetentur Caeli	ant.; Offertory, Christmas Day	Christmas
Tue Es Petrus	ant. St. Peter and Paul	St. Peter and Paul; General
Puer Natus	(Christmas carol)	Christmas
Salve Rex Noster	adapt. from Pentecost anthem of Bl. Virgin	General
Deus in Adjutorium	Ps. Maundy Thurs.; Sext, All Souls; etc.	General
Verbum Caro	ant. Christmas	Christmas; General